Beauty and the Image of God

"Finding true beauty within yourself."

Taryn V. Hudson

Copyright © 2024 Taryn V. Hudson
All rights reserved.

No part of this book may be reproduced or transmitted in any form or by any means, electronic or mechanical, including photocopying, recording, or by any information storage and retrieval system, without permission in writing from the copyright owner. Scripture quotations marked KJV are from the Holy Bible, King James Version (Authorized Version). First published in 1611. Quoted from the KJV Classis Reference Bible, Copyright © 1983 by the Zondervan Corporation. Scripture quotations marked AMP are from the Holy Bible, Amplified Version which was jointly produced by Zondervan and the Lockman Foundation. Scripture quotations marked ESV are from the Holy Bible, English Standard Version which was published in 2001 by Crossway. Scripture quotations marked NIV are from the New International Version which was published by Biblica and was released in 1978. A Minor revision was made in 1984 and a major revision was made in 2011.

ISBN: 979-8-218-39983-2

Contents

Dedication 1

Acknowledgment 3

Special Thanks 5

Foreword 7

Introduction 9

Chapter 1 What is Beauty? 11

Chapter 2 Mirror Mirror 17

Chapter 3 Auntie Knows Best 23

Chapter 4 Who Hurt You? 29

Chapter 5 Naked and Afraid 37

Chapter 6 I Look Like My Father 43

Chapter 7 New Me, Who Dis? 47

My Hope and Prayer For You 53

Follow the Author 55

Dedication

To start, I would like to thank the Lord above from the bottom of my heart. All Glory goes to God, and I am fully aware that without Him, I would not know myself and how dope I really am.

I would like to dedicate this book to my beautiful family, whom I love dearly, and to my amazing friends who have helped me throughout the years. Thank you all for believing in me. Without you all, I wouldn't have the courage to be the woman I am today. I pray that God reveals himself more to each of you and that He blesses you beyond your imagination.

Acknowledgment

I would like to acknowledge every single person who has been a part of my journey to self-worth and beauty. Every experience, both good and bad, has cultivated the path ahead of me. Therefore, I am thankful to those of you who have given me every bit of advice, encouragement, prayer, prophetic word, and patience.

Special Thanks

I would like to give a special thanks to Mrs. Connie Freeman for sharing her resources and encouragement. I would also like to thank Mrs. Gretchel Dixon for her assistance and her belief in my vision. I pray that you both experience many more blessings from our Lord above and that *"you may succeed and prosper and be in good health [physically], just a [I know] your soul prospers [spiritually]."* 3 John 1:2 (AMP)

Foreword

In a society habitually clouded with stereotypes, finding beauty becomes an act of great significance. It is a voyage that exceeds the conventional, guiding us to perceive the

extraordinary in the ordinary, the relevance in the seemingly irrelevant. This pursuit of beauty is not simply a quest for aesthetic gratification but a profound exploration of human experiences.

In this book, we board a voyage together—a journey that traverses landscapes seeking to expose the multiple forms of beauty surrounding us. The axiom that beauty is in the eye of the beholder helps us to reveal countless appearances and perceptions of beauty, inviting us to pause, contemplate, and marvel. In these pages, you will encounter stories, reflections, and insights from an individual who has embarked on her own journey of discovery. You'll read how each experience brings a unique perspective on finding beauty in a world filled with joy and sorrow.

As you immerse yourself in these words, I invite you to open your heart and mind to the possibility of beauty in all its forms. May this book inspire you to see the world with fresh eyes,

embrace the moments of wonder that surround you, and celebrate the profound beauty that infuses every aspect of life. For in the act of finding beauty, we discover something truly

extraordinary—that even in the darkest of times, there is always light to be seen, and even in the most mundane of moments, there is always magic waiting to be revealed.

I've had the privilege to marvel at the beautiful spirit of the author since 2011. Her intelligence, grace, spirituality, talents, and wisdom at a young age were to be admired. She is a true example of what embracement and serenity look like. These traits still hold true today. I invite you to unveil the magic of realizing your true beauty in the pages of this book.

With warmest regards,
JoAnn N. Scales, Ed.D

Introduction

Okay, so let me start off by saying that this is not an autobiography. However, this is my way of being vulnerable and sharing segments of my life with you while telling the story of how God has given me a reformed perspective of beauty and worth. This journey was one of much difficulty, confusion, heartbreak, and mental turmoil; nevertheless, the journey brought great clarity, understanding, and healing. I find great pleasure in sharing the gospel of beauty and how God saved me from horrific events, people, and even myself. This is MY gospel, and I wanted to share it with *you*. I hope this book serves as an outlet for you. God bless you, and I love you.

CHAPTER 1
What is Beauty?

The question of beauty never really seems to have a consistent answer. Probably because beauty is viewed differently by all of us. If you ask a person what they believe beauty is, they might give the cliché response of, "Beauty is in the eyes of the beholder", which is essentially a generic way of saying that beauty is subjective. Someone else might say, "Beauty comes from within", which indicates that your beauty is based on who you are as a person. If you ask Google, it will say that beauty is "a combination of qualities, such as shape, color, or form, that pleases the aesthetic senses, especially the sight", which is an utterly theoretic way of saying "pretty." This is not to say these statements are incorrect; each one of them is completely accurate in its own fashion. However, what does that even mean? How can we know what beauty really looks like? Most importantly, how do we determine where we fit into all of this?

The topic of beauty dates all the way back to the beginning of time. If we look back at ancient history, beauty had a lot to do with the symmetry of someone's face and their health. Women would adorn themselves with jewels, pearls, curls, fabrics, and fragrances that would make them appear more attractive to the public eye. Some women would even apply makeup to appear fairer and line their eyes with eyeliners made of charcoal. They would even use crushed berries and flowers to give color to their cheeks and lips. They would also alter their bodies by wearing tight corsets that made their figure appear more of an hourglass. These were some of the beauty

What is Beauty?

standards of our ancestors; however, history always has a way of repeating itself. These beauty routines that our mothers, grandmothers, and great-grandmothers had to make themselves appear beautiful are the same routines we include in our present-day lifestyles. But one thing we fail to realize is that this is simply an appearance.

My family and I used to live in a home off the highway headed toward Sherrill, Arkansas, which was THE country. When I was a young child between the ages of 8 and 11, I watched sitcoms on a television station called UPN—I know I just dated myself there. Some of my favorite shows on that station were The Parkers, That's So Raven, Living Single, and the list goes on and on. I can even remember fighting my brothers for the remote control just so I could indulge in the series of entertainment. I would sit on the couch in front of the wide 50-inch flatscreen television while wearing my little pink robe. Most likely, I had just finished cleaning the living room and vacuuming the carpet. Afterward, I would sit with a Hot Pocket and a wine glass filled with homemade Kool-Aid loaded with what we used to call "powdered diabetes", a.k.a sugar. We didn't have a lot of money, but that didn't mean I couldn't feel fancy while I watched TV. I used to laugh and admire the characters on the screen. The commonality of the sitcoms was that they all featured outrageously beautiful women of all shapes and sizes. Kim Parker, played by Countess Vaughn in "The Parkers," was not the ripest fruit on the tree. As a matter of fact, she was probably the overly ripened fruit that fell on the ground, and nobody wanted to eat it. However, she was a very talented singer and expressed her creativity through making clothing. Raven Baxter, played by Raven Symone, was the same type of influence for me at that time—plus-sized, beautiful, talented, and intuitive, which is how I also am. She inspired me to find new ways to style my clothes in a manner that flattered my full frame. And Khadijah James, played by Queen Latifah in "Living

Chapter 1

Single," displayed a level of confidence and strength that I had wished to have. She was business-oriented, serious, and was typically the person who regulated the home that she and her friends lived in. She was bold, a bit goofy, and didn't care what anyone thought of her. I esteemed that. I hate to say it, but at the time, these fictional characters were my idols. Therefore, I spent a tremendous amount of time trying to become like them instead of learning who I was. Time after time, I would forget that the characters were not the real celebrities. Therefore, I would fool myself into trying to become what they were pretending to be. The image they displayed on camera didn't even exist—it wasn't real life. They may have possessed a few of the attributes of their particular character; yet it was still a character. In fact, if you take a look at them in real life, they are absolutely nothing like their characters nor are they the ones people are to admire as Christians. They were simply acting.

Over the years, I've learned that it didn't matter how well I styled my clothes or how I wore my hair and makeup, what mattered most was what defined me. Clothes, hair, makeup, and jewelry only assist in creating an image—they are merely accessories. But the Spirit of God is what exudes beauty. God *is* beautiful. Now, you may wonder how is that possible when you cannot see Him. Let's take a look at Genesis 1:26-27(AMP) to get a better understanding of how God views us.

26) Then God said, "Let us (Father, Son, and the Holy Spirit) make man in Our image, according to Our likeness [not physical, but a spiritual personality and moral likeness]; and let them have complete authority over the fish of the sea, the birds of the air, the cattle, and over the entire earth, and over everything that creeps and crawls on the earth."

27) So God created man in His own image, in the image and likeness of God He created them.

What is Beauty?

God showed me that when He created man, He created us in His image. But oftentimes, we get this confused with an actual image. We think that to be in the image of God, we have to go make-up-free and look pale in the face when that is not what He is referring to. If that were the case, then you'd have to ask yourself again, "What does God look like?" Well, we understand that God is a spirit. He does not have a physical face. His physical representation was Jesus, but not everyone looks like Jesus. So, what does it mean to be in God's image? Look closely at verse twenty-six again. It reads, "and God said Let us make man in our image, after our likeness..." Notice how He says, "after *our* likeness" and not "*and* after our likeness." If He had said it that way, it would seem as though it was an addition instead of a description of His image. When God mentioned making man in His image, it simply means that He has given man His Spirit and His Characteristics. The only way you can take on God's image is to accept His son as your Lord and Savior and live according to the Word. The more you read the Word, the more you learn the personality of God, and, in turn, you learn about yourself. You will begin to see how beautiful God is through His scriptures, and then you will start to become the scriptures in the same manner as Jesus did in St. Luke 2:52(AMP). *"And Jesus kept increasing in wisdom and in stature, and in favor with God and men."*

Through Christ, you are already confident, creative, strong, intelligent, and wise. You don't have to be like any other created being, fictional or non-fictional, to have any of these qualities. You possess authentic qualities after you've been born again because that is how your Heavenly Father is. You are unique, You are fearfully, and wonderfully made as the Bible says in Psalms 139:14. With Him, it is effortless because you don't have to be what Google or society calls "pretty" to be beautiful. His glory gives us an indescribable glow. It is His Glow-ry! The Word that lives in you is BEAUTY!

Chapter 1

Heart Explorer: What was your definition of beauty before reading this passage? What is something about yourself that you believe makes you beautiful?

_____
_____
_____
_____
_____
_____
_____
_____
_____
_____
_____
_____
_____
_____
_____
_____
_____
_____
_____
_____
_____
_____
_____
_____
_____
_____
_____
_____
_____

What is Beauty?

CHAPTER 2
Mirror Mirror

Have you ever seen the movie "Overcomer"? If you haven't, I suggest you go check it out. It is one of those films I could watch repeatedly without getting tired of it. Anyway, there is a scene in the movie around the 39:00 minute mark where the blind patient is talking to the track coach while lying on a hospital bed. The blind man asked the coach, "Who are you?" which seems like a simple question, but it is far more complex than we think. The coach gave several different answers, but "Christian" was not listed until the very end of his response. After frustrating the coach with his inquisitive challenge, it was as if he had never even considered what could define him. The blind man goes on to say another one of the simplest yet most profound quotes I've ever heard:

"When you find your identity in the One who created you, it will change your whole perspective."

I can remember being 11 years old sitting at my baby-blue vanity while staring at myself in this huge round mirror sitting on top of it. I had already started puberty by the age of nine, so I was experiencing a lot of changes that I was unfamiliar with. I was one of the taller and bigger girls in middle school. I had adult-like assets that fooled several high schoolers. In my reflection, I could see my chocolatey acne-prone skin, chubby face with brown frames covering my eyes, fuller figure, and short curls saturated in Jheri curl activator that drenched my collar and pillows. I was not that appealing to my crushes because they took interest in my lighter-skinned, slimmer-figured friends who had longer, prettier hair, and

Mirror Mirror

nicer clothes. I recognized very quickly I was not the ideal choice for them based on what most of them would say was beautiful. There wasn't a day that went by where I wasn't called "fat," "ugly," "stupid," or even the more profane names I won't mention. However, one of the worst things I heard from someone I liked was "The only way I would go out with you is if I felt sorry for you." I know…that was VERY harsh. It lowered my self-esteem to the floor. What made it even worse was growing up with all brothers who would say the exact same things. I couldn't escape the verbal torture. So, all I would do was go to my bedroom and sit at my baby-blue vanity and cry. My perspective of myself was according to what they told me I was. And I believed them.

It was dark in my bedroom one night. I remember sitting on the edge of my twin-sized bed…thinking and crying. Reminiscing on the words that were haunting my 11-year-old mind, I could only think to myself, *"Why does everyone hate me? Why did God have to make me this way? Why can't I be like the other girls? I just want someone to like me. I'm tired of this."* I felt a dark presence in the room that was terrifying. "They don't care about you. They don't even like you. They would be better off without you. As a matter of fact, if you left now, they wouldn't even recognize that you were gone." That was all I could hear from that dark, evil presence. I sat there recollecting the words I heard while crying and holding my activator-drenched pillow to my face. I rocked back and forth hoping that no one could hear me sobbing. I listened intently to my family in the living room since my bedroom was close by. The walls were paper thin. I could hear them laughing, eating, and having a great time…without me. *"You're right. I bet if I'm gone, they would accept me."* I thought to myself as I agreed with the enemy. That was all I wanted—to be accepted. Suddenly, I took a mental glimpse of my funeral—seeing my family members crying and wishing things were different, but it was too late. I could see my picture above a white casket and

Chapter 2

devastation on their faces from my abrupt departure. Somehow, I became content with the evil presence that surrounded me. I figured that to ease my internal pain, I had to take physical action. My mother used to work at Walmart, and she kept her blue work vest on top of the dryer in the hallway conveniently near where my room was located. I snuck out of the room and grabbed the yellow and black box cutter hiding inside of her left vest pocket. I knew exactly where she would keep it because she was left-handed. I snuck back into my room and sat back on the edge of my bed, crying as quietly as I could. "It's ok. They won't even notice." Said the enemy. My perspective on life had shifted again. I was filled with anxiety; however, the idea of the pain ceasing overtook my young fragile mind. I just wanted to feel better even if it meant not feeling anything at all anymore. It was like I was at peace with the horrific idea. It's crazy how the enemy is so comforting when he's encouraging you to destroy yourself. Because not only are you destroying yourself physically, but you're destroying everything that you were created for when you were born. I was stuck in the moment though and I didn't care about what was ahead. I pushed the blade upward and directed it to my left wrist since my right hand was more dominant. My only hope was to cut a vital vein that led to my demise. However, as soon as the blade reached my wrist, I could feel pressure in my right arm as if someone were pushing it away. Suddenly, I heard a powerfully gentle voice yell, "Don't do it! I love you!" I tried to fight the pressure to pull away, but it was too strong. "Stop! I love you!" it said it again. There was a distinct difference between this voice and the dark voice. This voice was soothing, yet stern, like an authoritative figure. Have you ever been in a situation where you were so upset about something that you wanted to punch a wall, but then someone grabbed you and hugged you very tight to stop you? That's how *this* voice felt…like a hug. I dropped my hands and cried again because I just knew it had to be God, even though I didn't know Him at that point. That was the very first time I felt love that I could recognize. It was overwhelming. I didn't understand it because it was new to me. For the first time in my life, I felt wanted. I felt warmth, kindness, gentleness…joy. I didn't want to hurt myself anymore. But most of all, I didn't want anyone else to feel what I had felt. My perspective of life shifted once again. "I'm sorry, God," I mumbled under my maturing voice. I could feel the evil presence leaving my room. And all I could remember doing was crying myself to sleep. This time, my cry was soothing, and my sleep was peaceful.

Chapter 2

Heart Explorer: What was the moment in your life that made you realize that God was real? It doesn't have to be a traumatic experience; however, just take this moment to be honest and vulnerable with yourself.

_____
_____
_____
_____
_____
_____
_____
_____
_____
_____
_____
_____
_____
_____
_____
_____
_____
_____
_____
_____
_____
_____
_____
_____
_____
_____
_____

Mirror Mirror

CHAPTER 3
Auntie Knows Best

After school a few days later, I had to go spend the afternoon at my Aunt Thelma's house until my mom was off from work. For some strange reason, I was alone this time—my brothers weren't there which, now that I'm older, I understand why. There was a divine encounter that had to take place and I needed to be alone with her for it to happen the way God had ordained. My Aunt Thelma was one of my mom's older sisters. She lived in an apartment complex not too far from my mother's job at Walmart. She was bedridden, so she couldn't get around much without assistance; however, she was one of the wisest God-fearing women I knew. She would say things that would make you forget she was disabled. She was the type of woman who could have a normal, regular conversation with someone that would lowkey turn into a sermon. She was loud, funny, and had a strong low-octave voice with an Arkansas accent that felt so warm and comfy. But most of all, she loved Jesus and I admired that. I wanted to be wise just like her.

I was sitting on the flower-printed couch in her living room watching old reruns of Nickelodeon cartoons on her 40-inch box television. Then suddenly I heard, "Hey Muffin, come in here!" She was in her bedroom. Muffin was a nickname my father gave me when I was an infant. I rose from the couch with my black jacket and pink and white backpack still on my person. As I walked into her bedroom, which was slightly adjacent to the living room, she suggested that I sit in a chair right next to her bed. "What are you doing?" She asked.

Auntie Knows Best

"Nothing, just watching TV" I replied anxiously while twirling my fingers. She noticed that I was nervous, and I didn't know why I was there. I thought maybe I was in trouble even though I didn't do anything. My anxiety was very heavy when I was a kid. She asked, "What's wrong." "Nothing" I replied. She began to stare at me almost as if she could see right through me. She could sense that my temperament had shifted. Then she asked, "How are the kids at school treating you?" I paused long enough to conjure up the very common lie, "Everything is fine" not realizing that my handicapped auntie was also a human lie detector. I thought, *"How could she have possibly known that I was having problems with the kids at school?"* I began to worry. In the most loving and patient tone, she assured me by saying, "It's alright if you're not alright." I could feel a slight pressure in the forehead and my eyes began to well up with tears as I told her about my experiences at school and at home. "They said I was ugly, fat, and stupid and my crush doesn't like me," I mumbled. And in typical Thelma Brown fashion, she lifted her voice and said, "Baby, wait until you get a little older. You ain't going to like them either!" I covered my smile with my right hand and giggled a little. It was funny, but I only believed her partially regarding that. She calmly said, "I know you probably can't see it right now, but you are such a beautiful little girl. More importantly, you are the Lord's child. You are the apple of His eye, and He loves you so much." Her words reminded me of the voice I heard in my room. And the presence I felt in that moment was the same presence I felt then. "Reach over and hand me that Bible. I want to show you something." She spoke. "Yes, ma'am," I replied as I grabbed the black, worn-out Bible she had sitting on her nightstand. I could tell she read it often because some of the pages were slightly torn and the covers were cracking at the edges. "Read this." She demanded. I grabbed the book and gazed at the pages through my brown frames and thick lenses and read:

Chapter 3

"For you created my inmost being; you knit me together in my mother's womb. I praise you because I am fearfully and wonderfully made; your works are wonderful; I know that full well. My frame was not hidden from you when I was made in the secret place when I was woven together in the depths of the earth. Your eyes saw my unformed body; all the days ordained for me were written in your book before one of them came to be." Psalms 139: 13-16 (NIV)

After reading the passage, I wept while thinking about what almost took place a few days prior. It was all starting to make sense to me now. "You are smart, you are funny, and all that matters is who you are on the inside. God made you for a reason, and He has a plan for your life. He is the only One who knows everything about you. Don't let these little knucklehead boys tell you who you are." I began to cry even more because no one had ever encouraged me like that before. For once, I felt like my life meant something. "Go get me a pen and paper" she demanded. I respectfully replied, "Yes ma'am" and rushed to retrieve what she needed. She kept a pen and notebook next to her bed where her Bible had rested. I grabbed the pad and pen, handed them to her, and hopped back into the chair next to her bed. I was excited about the new revelation I had received. "What do you like about yourself?" she asked. I couldn't think of one word to describe anything positive. All I could remember was what was spoken over me. I started to get anxious again because I couldn't recall anything about myself that I was fond of. "I don't know" I replied. My voice began to crack, and my eyes became glossy. The only thoughts flowing through my mind were the lies I was told. "Breathe," Auntie said tranquilly. Her cello-like voice flowed like water. I took a short breath followed by a deeper, heavier breath. I could feel my heart rate decreasing. The more I stopped to breathe, the clearer my mind became. "Ok, let's try it a different way. What did you just read?" she asked. I was able to summon up a few words, "I am fearfully and wonderfully made." I said softly. "Ok, write that down!" she exclaimed, "What else?" I

Auntie Knows Best

paused, but only for a couple of seconds. "God created me before I was born, so I'm perfect just the way I am." "That's good! Write that down." She exclaimed. We sat in her room for about 30 minutes writing and reviewing my list according to what I read in the Bible. Toward the end of the conversation, she said, "Now, what I want you to remember is that you are beautiful, and you belong to the Lord. Can't nobody take that from you. Don't let anyone tell you what you ain't! Every time you look in your mirror, I want you to say what's written on this paper. Repeat it to yourself over and over again until you believe it." "Yes ma'am," I replied as she slowly handed me the loose sheet of paper. I stood up and leaned over her bed to give her a hug. Once again, my perspective of my life was shifted; however, this time, my perspective was more enlightened. I folded the paper, put it in the side pocket of my backpack, and kept it there until my mom came by to pick me up.

When I arrived home, I immediately ran into my room. It was much brighter in there this time. I sat on the stool at that big baby-blue vanity and stared at the reflection in that big round mirror and said these words to myself:

"I am beautiful. I am smart. I am kind. I am brave. I am loved. I am brilliant. I am fearfully and wonderfully made. God created me in the womb. I am capable of anything. I am the Lord's child. I am wise. My life is important. God loves me. He sees me. He knows me. When I see myself, I see Him. I am one of a kind and I belong here."

I had felt so empowered after reciting these truths to myself. There was an overwhelming amount of joy that came over me. For once, I felt like I could conquer anything. I finally felt a sense of confidence from this new revelation. However, I had no idea what was ahead of me. I had no clue that my life would change so drastically in the next few years. The thought that God would eventually put me to the test as a teenager was beyond my conception and I wasn't prepared to see my new reflection.

Chapter 3

Heart Explorer: What do you see when you look in the mirror? What are some things like about yourself? (Remember, it is ok if you can't think of anything. Take a moment and ask God to reveal yourself to you.)

Auntie Knows Best

CHAPTER 4
Who Hurt You?

Everyone has had their heart broken at some point in their lives. Whether it was by the death of a family member, friend, partner, spouse, betrayal, rejection, or whatever the case may be. We've all experienced it. For most of us, it's happened multiple times. Heartbreak is one of the most painful feelings a person can endure. As a matter of fact, according to www.heart.org, there is something called "Broken Heart Syndrome" which is also called stress-induced cardiomyopathy. This is when you feel intense chest pains that can be caused by an emotionally stressful occurrence. A heartbreak can sometimes feel like death. According to an article from www.unitypoint.org, a heartbreak can be proceeded by death if the brokenness hasn't subsided.

I remember my mom telling me a story about an elderly man from my hometown who had lost his wife. They had done everything together—traveled the world, started a family, had grandkids, etc. Well, unfortunately, the wife became very sick, and eventually she passed away. The elderly man was so distraught because he had lost his one true love, his best friend, the one person who had been that close to him since he was a teenager. His heart was so deeply broken that it began to fail. After only about a month later, the elderly man went home to join his wife in the presence of the Lord. It was a bitter-sweet story—painfully beautiful. I knew that whenever I get married, I wanted to be loved, truly just like that until I fall asleep forever. Now please understand that there is a huge difference between heartbreak caused by unintentional events such as this one and those that are intentional from someone you thought loved you.

It was the summer of 2007. I was 14 years old, and I was becoming a bit "hot in the britches" and "smelling myself" as the old folks used to say. My physical features were becoming more developed. I had bigger breasts and thicker thighs, so I just *knew* I would seem more attractive to boys at school. I can remember being outside with some of my friends after summer band camp. I would take a shower at my Aunt Sherry's house since she lived right down the street from the high school where we practiced. I would change into some skin-tight Faded Glory jeans and a blouse, put my black and blonde kinky twists into the ponytail, and spray on some Calgon Tahitian Orchid Body Mist to make me irresistible...well, at least I thought it would lol. I would meet up with a boy who was also in the marching band. He was around the same age as my older brother. What made it even worse was that my older brother didn't even like this guy, which was one of the many reasons behind the forbidden fraternization. So, to protect this man's identity, let's just call him "Randy." Randy and I were never intimate; However, he enjoyed having his way with me. As did I. I was still technically a virgin though. I enjoyed his attention because I had never experienced anything like it before. He had a way of making me feel like the prettiest girl in the school. I liked the way he would talk to me, hug me, and make me feel desired. He said everything that my brothers and other boys didn't say. His voice seemed so deep at the time. When he would whisper in my ear, it felt like a gentle stream of cool water in a dry desert, so calm and relaxing. His words were like a breeze on a hot summer day. He was wide and tall, so whenever he held me, it was like a blanket swaddling a small child. His lips were like pillows and His scent was of fresh linen and Old Spice. I used to steal his hoodie and just breathe in the scent while reminiscing about the previous events. I'll never forget the moment he told me he loved me. For the first

Chapter 4

time in my life, my reflection wasn't taunting me. I felt loved, accepted…beautiful. I wasn't denied access to his embrace. This high school senior made me feel as though I was on cloud nine and no one could snatch me down. Everything I felt from him almost replicated the feeling I got when I first met God, but it was very different. It was tangible. Slowly, I began to worship that counterfeit feeling of intimacy to the point where I would do anything for it—literally ANYTHING. Sacrificing my own morals and happiness became normal if it meant I'd have an hour with Randy, or even a few minutes. I was so in love with this feeling and, for once, I didn't have to compete with the prettier girls for his affection—or at least I *thought* I didn't. Not once did I ever think I'd get the rudest awakening of all time.

It was a Friday night, which meant that Randy and I would be playing in the stands at a football game together. I was technically still in middle school, but some of the middle schoolers got a chance to play in the high school marching band if they were talented enough. The band bus would pick us up from the middle school and take us to the high school early enough to practice, eat, and get ready for the game. I got off the bus and headed straight to the nearest dollar store. I had used the remainder of the allowance my dad gave me to buy Randy a card and some candy. Making sure that the card was empty on the inside, I had written down my feelings so I could show him how much I loved him. I was a bit skilled at drawing, so I even drew a picture of us hugging each other. It was such a cute little card, and I couldn't wait to give it to him. I just *knew* he was going to love it because he loved me, right? Well, as soon as I stepped foot on campus, I looked and saw him walking. "Randy!" I yelled, He waved, but he kept walking with his uniform hanging halfway on his body. Giving him the benefit of the doubt, I thought *"Maybe he's in a hurry and needed to go somewhere."* So, I completely disregarded it until I got up the steps near the band room.

Who Hurt You?

That's when I saw it. He was hugged up with another girl who was also in the marching band. She was a bit older than me but younger than him. He held her the exact same way he would hold me. And, unfortunately, I witnessed him kiss her the exact same way he would kiss me. My heart sank to the ground—I felt deeply betrayed. It was like I was small and invisible like he didn't care how that would make me feel. Once he finished fooling with her, he walked back towards the band room. He saw me still standing there, disappointed and confounded. Then had the nerve to smile at me and yell, "Hey boo!" I had never rolled my eyes so hard in my life. I ran into the band room and cried while hiding in the bathroom. My heart was utterly broken, and I began to question myself, "What's wrong with *me*? What does she have that I don't? What's so bad about me that he had to find someone else? Why would he do this to me?" The man that I thought was the love of my 14-year-old life had deceived me. I ripped the card into shreds and tossed it in the trashcan. That was the very first time I had experienced heartbreak in that manner. And even though I was very young, I somehow understood that nobody could give me the same feeling that God gave me. No one could really love me like Him. Somehow, I understood the concept of forgiveness without fully grasping how to translate it verbally.

Now I'm the type of person who believes in Jesus and therapy. Back in 2021 during one of my sessions, my therapist took me through an exercise that forced me to relive the pain I had experienced in order to recognize the lesson in it. She had me write down whatever I had gone through and then write down what I gained from it. When I recalled the situation with Randy, I learned that even though there are people who don't care about your feelings, there are so many others around you who do. I now understand that not everyone was out to hurt me and that I didn't have to be afraid to let someone truly love me. I've also learned that God is the type of Father who would

Chapter 4

never hurt His children, But He would hurt someone for His children. If you look at Romans 12:19(ESV), Paul writes:

"Beloved, never avenge yourselves, but leave it to the wrath of God, for it is written, 'Vengeance is mine, I will repay, says the Lord.'"

You can forgive someone and still feel pain. However, we must understand that people are flawed; even those who are very close to us. Therefore, everyone is going to hurt you at some point in your life. *YOU* will hurt someone if you haven't done so already because you are also flawed. Some pain will be intentional, and others might be unintentional. All of it must be forgiven. Forgiveness allows you to feel pain while not holding a grudge or withholding anger against someone who has wronged you. Colossians 3:13(AMP) *"bearing graciously with one another, and willingly forgiving each other if one as a cause for complaint against another, just as the Lord has forgiven you, so should you forgive"*. Additionally, we cannot allow our pain to determine our worth. Never internalize the hurt you've endured by thinking "Maybe I wasn't this or that enough" or "If I would have done this or that, they would not have hurt me" or even "Maybe I should have accepted this or that." NO! Do not reduce your morals, boundaries, or values to please anyone. If they want you to reduce yourself from what God called you to, their time with you must be reduced. Period.

Who Hurt You?

Heart Explorer: At what point in your life did you experience such pain that it caused you to question your worth? What did you learn from that experience?

_____
_____
_____
_____
_____
_____
_____
_____
_____
_____
_____
_____
_____
_____
_____
_____
_____
_____
_____
_____
_____
_____
_____
_____
_____
_____
_____

Chapter 4

CHAPTER 5
Naked and Afraid

Constantly, I come in contact with people who talk about what being holy is and what a true man or woman of God looks like. They say you are holy if you wear long skirts, turtlenecks, suits, closed-toe shoes, no makeup, little to no jewelry, certain hairstyles that are not overly flattering, or haircuts with no beards—things like that. Now don't get me wrong, the Bible does say in 1 Timothy 2:9-10 (ESV) that *"women should adorn themselves in respectable apparel, with modesty and self-control, not with braided hair and gold or pearls or costly attire, but with what is proper for women who profess godliness—with good works."* The word "adorn" means "to decorate, embellish, or accessorize." He is not saying that we are not holy if we wear our hair a certain way or if we wear jewelry. He is saying that we should not allow what we wear or how we look to define our holiness. The last time I checked, a demon does not flee from you just because you aren't wearing lipstick. No one is holier than another because of their appearance. If you look closely at verse ten, he says "…with good works." Meaning that what you do to glorify God is what defines you. I cannot tell you how many wicked people I've met who look like what is considered to be Holy; however, their Christian counterparts who are covered in piercings and tattoos look far from Holy, yet they are the ones who are genuinely after God's own heart. Many of them have brought more people to Christ than those who are judged by their appearances alone.

Naked and Afraid

When I was around the age of twenty-four, I remember being called a harlot, all because my dress was slightly above my knees. Actually, they said verbatim, "You don't want to come off as a church hoe." That shocked me coming from someone I considered a friend. Meanwhile, the other young ladies who were dressed modestly were doing the most dirt behind closed doors. I didn't want to be inauthentic and use the appearance of holiness as a "cover-up." I was far from perfect and I still am. As a matter of fact, I liked showing a little leg, a bit of shoulder, and pedicured toes in my heels because I thought they were pretty. Especially, since I had learned how to accept my body as beautiful. Not once was I dressed in a disrespectful manner. Most of my figure was fully covered. Back then, I used to carry the mindset of "If anyone is tempted or offended by how I look, that's their fault!" The Bible does say that *"each person is tempted when they are lured and enticed by his own desire."* James 1:14 (ESV) If a person can look at someone with impure thoughts, their mind must be renewed. However, we should never intentionally do anything that could tempt anyone. The Bible also says in Matthew 18:6 (ESV) that *"whoever causes one of my little ones to sin, it would be better for him to have a great millstone tied to his neck and be drowned in the depth of the sea."* It's like dangling a piece of fried chicken in front of a fasting saint. Once I changed my perspective on modesty, I was able to style myself in a way that covered me but also made me feel gorgeous.

Now, you're probably wondering "What in the world does this have to do with being Naked and Afraid" Let me explain. There is a level of nakedness you must have as a Christian no matter how covered you may think you are. When I say "nakedness," I mean "vulnerability; exposure; openness." I learned that sometimes you have to get "naked" to see how uniquely beautiful you are. Many of us adorn ourselves according to the Word of God and we put on the appearance of holiness; but, for some of us, not once have we

Chapter 5

allowed ourselves to be naked before God because we are afraid. Vulnerability, even towards God, can be scary. It requires you to expose the innermost parts of yourself that have been covered by a smile, a joke, an outfit, money, etc. But nothing stays covered for long. I took this concept literally and figuratively. There were times when I was getting undressed and as I stood looking in the mirror, I began to admire every perfectly imperfect part of myself. I knew that if I had a visual representation of vulnerability that I wasn't afraid of, it would help me be more vulnerable in every other aspect of life.

I can recall the first time God asked me to expose myself. He was simply asking me to give Him my heart; however, the last time I gave my heart to someone, they broke it. It was still fragile. But then, He told me to give Him the broken pieces of my heart and He would put them back together. It was and still is a process. It showed me that, because of my brokenness, I would do things to ease the pain such as wearing clothes that exposed parts of my body. God shows me all the time, that when I dare to be naked before Him, He covers me and all of my brokenness. That encouraged me to honor Him by covering myself physically and to love myself the way He loves me.

Naked and Afraid

Heart Explorer: When was the last time you were naked before God? What did you discover in that moment? How did it change your perspective on modesty?

_____
_____
_____
_____
_____
_____
_____
_____
_____
_____
_____
_____
_____
_____
_____
_____
_____
_____
_____
_____
_____
_____
_____
_____
_____
_____
_____
_____
_____
_____

Chapter 5

CHAPTER 6
I Look Like My Father

When you were born, you were made in the image of your parents. But have you ever noticed how someone can look like their parents, but not exactly like them? Don't get me wrong, some people seem to be a spitting image of their parents, however, they are nothing like them. There is always something about them that is slightly different, good or bad.

I'll use myself as an example; I don't look exactly like either of my parents. As a matter of fact, I consider myself to be a beautifully blended combination of the two. My mother is absolutely gorgeous—beautiful olive skin that's a few shades lighter than mine and a jovial personality that anyone could love. I have some of her features like her nose, cheekbones, and eyelids, and I even have her voice. When I'm around her, I look like her but not quite. The same goes for my dad. He's a very handsome fellow with a dark bronze skin tone that is similar to my own. I also have some of his other features like his lips, eyebrows, and even some of his mannerisms. When I'm around him, I look just like him but still not quite. Neither of them looks alike, but they were able to create a group of people who are an embodiment of both of them. There are characteristics I have though that make anyone who knows me say "Girl, you are just like your momma or daddy." They can tell who my parents are based on my behavior—the way I laugh, the way I talk, my facial expressions, etc. Though I don't look exactly like them, what's within me embodies a reflection of who they are along with a splash of my own characteristics.

I Look Like My Father

Have you ever noticed how a compliment from your mother feels different from a compliment from your father? I know that it is different for each gender; however, there is something special about when a father calls his daughter beautiful. Any young lady who has experienced this knows that when a father or father figure compliments her, it brings about a sense of confidence that no one can take away. It's almost similar to when you're a teenager and a boy calls you beautiful for the first time—you tend to cling to him a little more than others. I remember when my dad called me "pretty girl" when I was roughly 15 or 16. I was sitting on a burgundy floral couch in the living room watching TV and he said verbatim, "Look at my pretty girl! Skin just glowing." It just hit differently, almost as if I had gained a new revelation of myself. Everything that I was told before that moment seemed to no longer exist. I remembered staring at myself in that same big light-blue vanity and admiring my skin, which was the same color as his. It did glow…and it was stunning. The sudden shift of my perspective allowed me to see the beauty in what I thought made me unattractive. I could finally see what he saw, and I loved it.

This is what God is talking about in Genesis 1:26 (KJV) when he said, *"Let us make man in our image, after our likeness…"* When you are born again, you are made in the image of God and your physical appearance does change to some extent. You will start acting more like Him because your characteristics begin to change according to what you've read in His Word. When you have received the fullness of the Holy Spirit, He will start to radiate through you, and you will begin to see what He sees. What's in you will show that you are in His image. When you speak, laugh, walk, etc., others will be able to tell who your Father is.

Chapter 6

Heart Explorer: What are some of the positive features or characteristics that you have acquired from your parents? What are some things or characteristics that you have displayed that show others that God is real in YOU?

_____
_____
_____
_____
_____
_____
_____
_____
_____
_____
_____
_____
_____
_____
_____
_____
_____
_____
_____
_____
_____
_____
_____
_____
_____

I Look Like My Father

CHAPTER 7
New Me, Who Dis?

When I got saved in college at the age of nineteen, I noticed I had become more attractive to both Christians and counterfeits. I was growing up and becoming more appealing, which made having relationships more difficult. Therefore, I had to learn how to discern between the two which resulted in taking authority over what I would allow. In Genesis 1:26 (KJV) God says, *"... let them have dominion over the fish of the sea, over the fowl of the air, and over the cattle, and over all the Earth, and over every creeping thing that creeps upon the Earth."* These are the things that God did; therefore he wants us to do them, as well. Any good parent would want their children to be a reflection of their goodness and how they raised them. I was happy to be a part of His family. I liked being a Christian, but I also liked being liked which turned me into a serial (now former) people-pleaser. One of the most difficult lessons I learned was setting boundaries, and that took time.

Anyone who knows me well knows that I have been in some pretty atrocious relationships and friendships, all because I didn't know how to end things. I was terrible at walking away from anything that wasn't working, for the sake of being understood, and loyal. However, I had to learn that I was harming myself more by staying close to anyone who didn't have my best interest at heart. I remember when I was in an eight-year on-again/off-again relationship with a very toxic person who claimed to be a man of God. Let's call him "Patrick." You see, Patrick was charming with his words, and he knew exactly how to get your hopes up. However,

New Me, Who Dis?

while I was with him, I learned that he was abusive and narcissistic. As a matter of fact, he was the first person to ever show me what spiritual abuse was. If you are not sure what that is, it is when someone uses your religious beliefs to gain control over you. They will play on your emotions or manipulate you into thinking that if you do not obey them, then you are not obeying God. There are several pastors who are doing that very thing today, but that's another topic for another day. Anyway, Patrick always knew exactly what to do or say to keep me under his spell. I was constantly going back to him, even after he hurt me. It felt almost like I was dating the devil himself. And even though I knew that dealing with him was wrong, it always felt right. My discernment went out of the window. I didn't realize that I was being abused until a close friend pointed it out at the time; however, like most abuse survivors, I didn't want to believe that I had endured such a thing. But eventually, I had to face reality. The final straw wasn't until I reached the age of 26 in 2019. We were in another "off-again" stage of our relationship; therefore I decided to start seeing other people. I started dating a cute little African guy, and that made Patrick furious to the point where he harassed both of us. He would stalk us, and call us in the wee hours of the night. Patrick even harassed my family members just to get in touch with me. I was so drained by the way my life was going when I realized that I didn't have to accept it any longer. So, with a little help from my new boo at the time and some family members, I did everything in my power to get as far away from Patrick as possible. I moved away, got a restraining order, and blocked him on every social media platform I could think of. Finally, I was free from the turmoil and ready to embark on a new journey.

It was in 2021 when my relationship with the new boo ended. That was probably one of the most devastating breakups that I had experienced, especially because he was with me during the most traumatic time of my life. I managed to get over it with the help of

Chapter 7

plenty of therapy, church, and new beautiful life experiences. One of the many lessons I learned in therapy is that sometimes we think we are in love with someone when in actuality we love how they supported us during our difficulties. The major trigger for me during that time was being told to let go. It was because I wanted to hold on to what I thought provided me comfort and safety. I learned that I had to let go to receive something new. So once I let go of who I thought was the love of my life, I was able to receive something even greater—myself.

You cannot love anyone more than you love yourself and you cannot love yourself more than you love God. Even if you try to, eventually you will realize that even the love you have for yourself is limited. When you put others' needs before your own, you break boundaries and do things that you may regret later. But when you love God first before everything, you will realize that love starts wherever He is. Also, I knew that I had to let go of who I used to be to appreciate who I am now. The moment I began to love God was the moment I began to love myself more. One of my favorite books of all time is "The Gift of Being Yourself" by David E. Benner and one of my favorite quotes from that book is:

"Paradoxically, as we become more and more like Christ we become more uniquely our own true self."

When we become a new creation in Christ, we are actually going back to who he created us to be in the first place. However, this is a new discovery for us, which is why we must be born again. When we are babies, we are unaware of how the world will shape and shift us into what it wants us to be. Therefore, we have to be reborn into the life that was originally set in place for us. Once we are born again, we become unrecognizable even to ourselves. So don't be surprised if your demeanor changes and you start doing things you never thought you would do. Just thank God and know that it is for the best.

New Me, Who Dis?

Heart Explorer: What have you experienced in your life that showed you that you needed a change? How has God shifted your way of seeing yourself? What are some things you do now for your benefit that you didn't do in the past?

_____
_____
_____
_____
_____
_____
_____
_____
_____
_____
_____
_____
_____
_____
_____
_____
_____
_____
_____
_____
_____
_____
_____
_____
_____
_____
_____

Chapter 7

My Hope and Prayer For You

I sincerely hope that this book has been a blessing to you and that you have received something that you can use now or in the future. I also hope that my sharing my story has helped you to realize that you are not alone. We all have a journey that we are walking out, and it does not end until we do. My prayer for you is that you understand how much God loves you. You are going through your journey so that others can see the beauty of God through you. I know it may be difficult to see at the moment, but He is revealing Himself to you and through you even at this very moment. I pray that God opens your eyes to recognize how beautiful you are and that He will never put you on a path to harm you, but to give you hope and a future. I cancel every lie from the enemy, and I speak life over you. You are fearfully and wonderfully made, and I decree and declare that this is only the beginning of the best moments of your life. In Jesus Holy name I pray, Amen.

Follow the Author

Instagram: @_tarynvh

Facebook: Taryn Hudson

TikTok: @tarynvairl

www.ingramcontent.com/pod-product-compliance
Lightning Source LLC
Chambersburg PA
CBHW072035060426
42449CB00010BA/2266